SAINT BERNARDS

FAVORITE DOG BREEDS

Dan Lopez

NorwoodHouse Press

Cataloging-in-Publication Data

Names: Lopez, Dan.
Title: St. Bernards / Dan Lopez.
Description: Buffalo, NY : Norwood House Press, 2026. | Series: Favorite dog breeds| Includes glossary and index.
Identifiers: ISBN 9781978576650 (pbk.) | ISBN 9781978576667 (library bound) | ISBN 9781978576674 (ebook)
Subjects: LCSH: Saint Bernard dog--Juvenile literature.
Classification: LCC SF429.S3 L67 2026 | DDC 636.73--dc23

Published in 2026 by
Norwood House Press
2544 Clinton Street
Buffalo, NY 14224

Designer: Rhea Magaro
Editor: Kim Thompson

Photo credits: Cover, p. 1 Aneta Jungerova, Giraphics/Shutterstock.com; p. 4, 14 Wikipedia.com; p. 5 Rita_Kochmarjova/Shutterstock.com; p. 6 Rita_Kochmarjova/Shutterstock.com; p. 8, 9 Rita_Kochmarjova/Shutterstock.com; p. 10 Schwabenblitz/Shutterstock.com; p. 15 Zeutschel Omniscan 12/Shutterstock.com; p. 17 KAZLOVA IRYNA/Shutterstock.com; p. 18 Becky Swora/Shutterstock.com; p. 19 Sebw/Shutterstock.com; p. 20 Andrii Anna photographers/Shutterstock.com; p. 21 Jota Buyinch Photo/Shutterstock.com

Printed in the United States of America

CPSIA compliance information: Batch #CWNHP26: For further information contact Norwood House Press at 1-800-237-9932.

TABLE OF CONTENTS

Meet the Saint Bernard

Saint Bernards are popular pets. Dogs of this **breed** are known for their size and strength and for their history of rescuing people on snowy mountaintops.

A Saint Bernard is the star of the movie *Beethoven*.

What Do Saint Bernards Look Like?

Saint Bernards are huge! Adults can stand 30 inches (76 centimeters) tall. They can weigh 200 pounds (90 kilograms).

This **muscular** dog has a big head with a short **muzzle**. It has a big, **sensitive** nose. It walks with a slow, heavy **gait**. It drools a lot!

A Saint Bernard's **dense** fur can be short or medium in length.

All Saint Bernards are reddish-brown, black, and white.

Where Do Saint Bernards Come From?

Saint Bernards come from the country of Switzerland, which is covered by towering mountains called the Alps. Hundreds of years ago, the dogs were raised to work on farms.

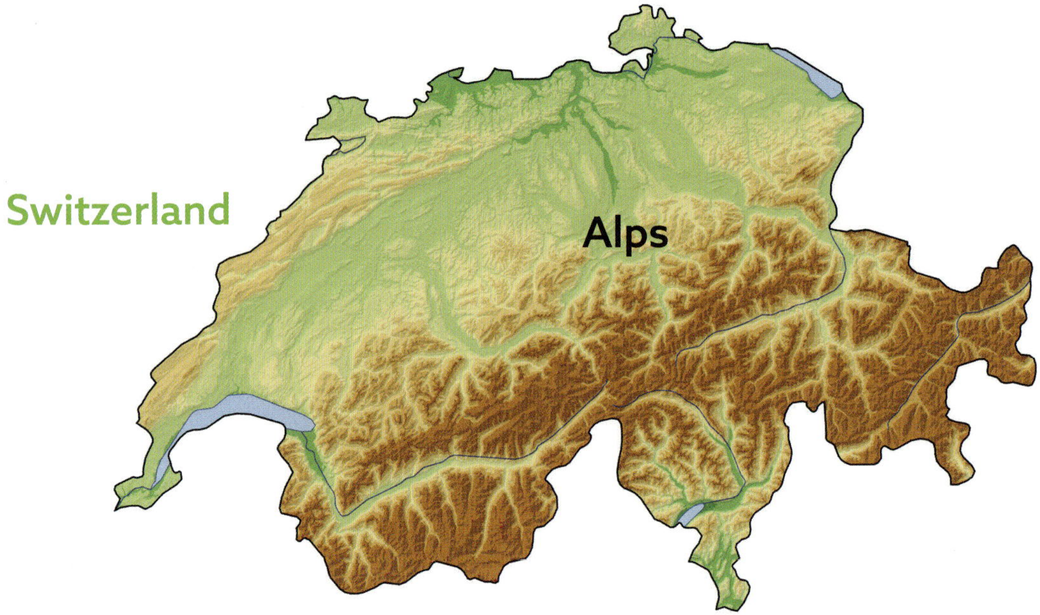

Saint Bernards get their name from a high, snowy, dangerous place in the Alps called Great Saint Bernard Pass. Long ago, **monks** set up a hospital there. They trained the dogs to sniff out people who got lost in the mountains or buried by **avalanches**.

Over the years, Saint Bernards rescued thousands of people in the Alps. A dog named Barry became famous for helping nearly 50 people.

A famous painting showed a Saint Bernard with a small wooden barrel on its collar for carrying supplies to lost travelers. The dogs did not really do this, but the painting made people think it was true.

Do Saint Bernards Make Good Pets?

Saint Bernards make great pets. These gentle giants are smart and friendly. They are very **patient**. They get along well with kids.

Saint Bernards like to play, but they do not need a lot of exercise.

They like cold weather best. They do not like to be outside in the hot sun.

What Do Saint Bernards Need?

A Saint Bernard has a big **appetite**. It needs lots of food!

These dogs need regular brushing to keep their coats smooth and clean.

Glossary

appetite (AP-uh-tite): desire for food

avalanches (AV-uh-lan-chis): times when large masses of snow and ice break loose and fall down the side of a mountain

breed (breed): one type or kind of an animal

dense (dens): thick

gait (gayt): way of walking

monks (muhngks): men who live apart from others in religious communities

muscular (MUHS-kyuh-lur): having strong muscles

muzzle (MUHZ-uhl): the nose and mouth of an animal

patient (PAY-shuhnt): able to put up with things without getting angry or upset

sensitive (SEN-si-tiv): able to notice or feel things easily

Thinking Questions

1. Describe a Saint Bernard's fur.
2. What is Switzerland like?
3. Where did Saint Bernards get their name?
4. Who was Barry?
5. Why do you think Saint Bernards dislike hot weather?

Index

About the Author

Dan Lopez is a writer who loves dogs! He has a German shepherd named Hans and an Irish setter named Tam. They love to go for walks in the woods together. Sometimes, they jump in the lake for a swim. Dan lives in Indiana with his wife and three kids.